LOS ANGELES RAMS

BRENDAN FLYNN

WWW.APEXEDITIONS.COM

Copyright © 2025 by Apex Editions, Mendota Heights, MN 55120. All rights reserved. No part of this book may be reproduced or utilized in any form or by any means without written permission from the publisher.

Apex is distributed by North Star Editions:
sales@northstareditions.com | 888-417-0195

Produced for Apex by Red Line Editorial.

Photographs ©: Kevin Terrell/AP Images, cover, 1, 30–31, 47; Jayne Kamin-Oncea/Getty Images Sport/Getty Images, 4–5; Nic Antaya/Getty Images Sport/Getty Images, 6–7; Bettmann/Getty Images, 8–9, 10–11, 12–13; Charles Aqua Viva/Getty Images Sport/Getty Images, 14–15; Focus on Sport/Getty Images Sport/Getty Images, 16–17, 24–25, 34–35; Tony Tomsic/AP Images, 19, 57; Vic Stein/Getty Images Sport/Getty Images, 20–21, 22–23; Peter Brouillet/Getty Images Sport/Getty Images, 26–27; E. Bakke/Getty Images Sport/Getty Images, 28–29; Brian Bahr/Allsport/Getty Images Sport/Getty Images, 32–33; David Madison/Getty Images Sport/Getty Images, 37; Joe Robbins/AP Images, 38–39, 58–59; Elsa/Getty Images Sport/Getty Images, 40–41; John McCoy/Getty Images Sport/Getty Images, 42–43; Gregory Shamus/Getty Images Sport/Getty Images, 44–45; iStockphoto, 48–49; Vic Stein/AP Images, 50–51; Thearon W. Henderson/Getty Images Sport/Getty Images, 52–53; Bernstein Associates/Getty Images Sport/Getty Images, 54–55

Library of Congress Control Number: 2023922838

ISBN
979-8-89250-154-5 (hardcover)
979-8-89250-171-2 (paperback)
979-8-89250-295-5 (ebook pdf)
979-8-89250-188-0 (hosted ebook)

Printed in the United States of America
Mankato, MN
012025

NOTE TO PARENTS AND EDUCATORS

Apex books are designed to build literacy skills in striving readers. Exciting, high-interest content attracts and holds readers' attention. The text is carefully leveled to allow students to achieve success quickly.

TABLE OF CONTENTS

CHAPTER 1
RAMS' HOUSE! 4

CHAPTER 2
EARLY HISTORY 8

PLAYER SPOTLIGHT
DEACON JONES 18

CHAPTER 3
LEGENDS 20

CHAPTER 4
RECENT HISTORY 28

PLAYER SPOTLIGHT
KURT WARNER 36

CHAPTER 5
MODERN STARS 38

PLAYER SPOTLIGHT
AARON DONALD 46

CHAPTER 6
TEAM TRIVIA 48

TEAM RECORDS • 56
TIMELINE • 58
COMPREHENSION QUESTIONS • 60
GLOSSARY • 62
TO LEARN MORE • 63
ABOUT THE AUTHOR • 63
INDEX • 64

RAMS' HOUSE!

Music pumps through the stadium. Bright lights flash. The fans rise to their feet. The announcer fires up the crowd. Soon, the players run onto the field. It's time for Los Angeles Rams football!

The Rams' stadium can hold more than 70,000 football fans.

Rams quarterback Matthew Stafford takes the snap. Defenders crash in. But Stafford gets away. Then he spots an open receiver. He launches a deep pass. Puka Nacua catches it. He runs into the end zone. It's a touchdown!

WHOSE HOUSE?

Rams fans do a cheer during games. The announcer shouts, "Whose house?" Then the crowd yells, "Rams' house!" The cheer is based on a song from the 1980s. Hip-hop group Run-DMC had a hit called "Run's House."

Wide receiver Puka Nacua led the Rams in touchdown catches in 2023.

CHAPTER 2
EARLY HISTORY

The Rams formed in 1936. At first, they were based in Cleveland, Ohio. They played in a league called the AFL. That league didn't last long. In 1937, the Rams joined the NFL.

The Cleveland Rams offense poses for a photo in 1941.

The Rams weren't very good at first. But they put it all together in 1945. The Rams went 9–1 that year. Then they beat Washington to win the NFL title. That turned out to be their last game in Cleveland. In 1946, the Rams moved to Los Angeles, California.

COAST TO COAST

In 1946, the NFL became the first major sports league with a team on the West Coast. MLB didn't have any teams there until 1958. The NBA reached the West Coast in 1960. And the NHL added its first West Coast teams in 1967.

Jim Benton (49) led the NFL in receiving yards in 1945 and 1946.

The Rams were a big hit in Los Angeles. They reached the NFL title game in 1949 and 1950. But they lost both times. In 1951, they reached the title game again. This time, the Rams came out on top. They beat the Cleveland Browns 24–17.

BIG CROWDS

The Rams played their home games at the Los Angeles Coliseum. The stadium could hold more than 100,000 fans. By 1949, the Rams were leading the NFL in attendance. In 1957, a Rams game set a record. More than 102,000 fans filled the stands.

Dan Towler (32) ran for 36 yards and a touchdown in the 1951 title game.

John Cappelletti (22) breaks a tackle in a 1975 game against the San Diego Chargers.

Los Angeles had some excellent teams in the 1970s. The Rams won their division seven years in a row. They reached the conference title game five times. However, they lost the first four.

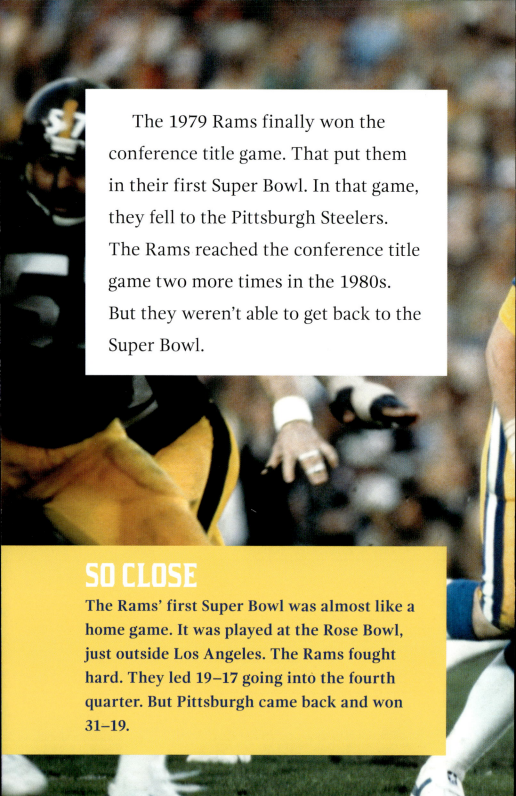

The 1979 Rams finally won the conference title game. That put them in their first Super Bowl. In that game, they fell to the Pittsburgh Steelers. The Rams reached the conference title game two more times in the 1980s. But they weren't able to get back to the Super Bowl.

SO CLOSE

The Rams' first Super Bowl was almost like a home game. It was played at the Rose Bowl, just outside Los Angeles. The Rams fought hard. They led 19–17 going into the fourth quarter. But Pittsburgh came back and won 31–19.

Mike Fanning (79) chases down Steelers quarterback Terry Bradshaw in the Super Bowl.

PLAYER SPOTLIGHT

DEACON JONES

Deacon Jones was one of the greatest pass rushers of all time. He joined the Rams as a rookie in 1961. Before long, he was starting at defensive end. Fans called the team's defensive line the "Fearsome Foursome."

Jones was quick for a player his size. He could blow past blockers. He could also overpower them. Jones led the NFL in sacks five times. Two of his best seasons came in 1964 and 1968. Both years, he recorded 22 sacks.

DEACON JONES HAD EIGHT SEASONS WITH 12 OR MORE SACKS.

CHAPTER 3

LEGENDS

The Rams had two great quarterbacks in their early years. Bob Waterfield was a rookie in 1945. He led the team to the NFL title that year. Later, he shared time with Norm Van Brocklin. Van Brocklin passed for 554 yards in a 1951 game. That set an NFL record.

Tom Fears (55), Bob Waterfield (7), and Norm Van Brocklin (25) study a play during a 1951 practice.

The Rams also had excellent wide receivers. Tom Fears led the NFL in catches in each of his first three seasons. That included 84 catches in 1950. The next year, Elroy "Crazy Legs" Hirsch set a record. He racked up 1,495 receiving yards that season.

'60s COMBO

Quarterback Roman Gabriel made the Pro Bowl three times in the 1960s. And in 1969, he earned the Most Valuable Player (MVP) Award. Gabriel's favorite target was Jack Snow. The wide receiver averaged 26.3 yards per catch in 1967.

Tom Fears led the NFL with 1,116 receiving yards in 1950.

The Rams have a history of strong defensive lines. In the 1960s, Deacon Jones and Lamar Lundy rushed from the ends. Merlin Olsen and Rosey Grier played in the middle. This "Fearsome Foursome" stuffed the run.

In the 1970s, Jack Youngblood became the team's defensive star. Youngblood led the NFL in sacks twice. He also made the Pro Bowl seven years in a row.

Jack Youngblood (85) played through the 1979 playoffs with a broken leg.

Eric Dickerson (29) won the Offensive Player of the Year Award in 1986.

In the 1980s, running back Eric Dickerson topped 1,800 yards three times. His best season came in 1984. He set an NFL record with 2,105 rushing yards. Quarterback Jim Everett spent only eight seasons in Los Angeles. Even so, he became the team's all-time passing leader.

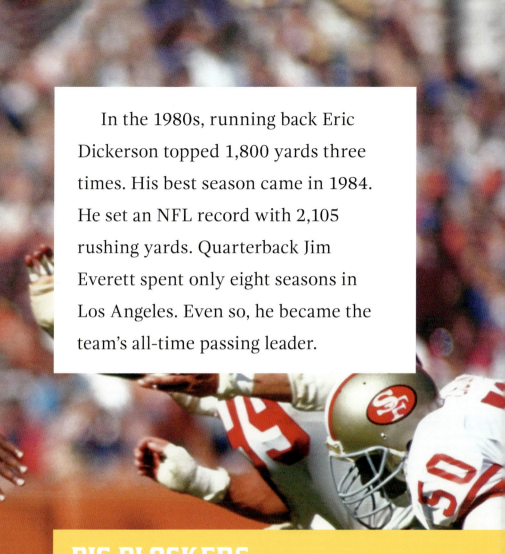

BIG BLOCKERS

The Rams had two of the best blockers ever. In the 1960s and 1970s, left guard Tom Mack led the way. He went to the Pro Bowl 11 times. Right tackle Jackie Slater joined the Rams in 1976. He spent 20 years with the team. Slater made the Pro Bowl seven times.

CHAPTER 4

RECENT HISTORY

The early 1990s were tough years for the Rams. They struggled on the field. And they didn't get the stadium improvements they wanted. So, in 1995, the team moved to St. Louis, Missouri.

Running back Jerome Bettis (36) won the Offensive Rookie of the Year Award in 1993.

Mike Jones tackles Titans receiver Kevin Dyson a yard short of the end zone to secure a Super Bowl win.

A new stadium opened during the team's first year in St. Louis. By their fifth season there, the Rams were ready to shake up the NFL. Their offense broke records. The team rolled into the Super Bowl. In that game, the Rams beat the Tennessee Titans 23–16.

HUGE STOP

The Super Bowl ended on an amazing play. The Titans had the ball. They needed a touchdown to tie the game. A Titans receiver caught a pass. He got to the 1-yard line. But Rams linebacker Mike Jones tackled him. The Rams were champions!

The Rams' offense led the NFL in points in 1999, 2000, and 2001.

The Rams made the playoffs four more times in the next five seasons. But after that, the team struggled. Beginning in 2005, the Rams missed the playoffs 11 years in a row. By then, the team's owner was planning to move back to Los Angeles. The team made the move in 2016.

TOUGH LOSS

In 2001, the Rams reached the Super Bowl for the second time in three years. They faced the New England Patriots. The Patriots led 17–3 going into the fourth quarter. The Rams came back and tied the game. But the Patriots won on a last-second field goal.

Aaron Donald (99) celebrates after sacking Bengals quarterback Joe Burrow in the Super Bowl.

In the 2018 season, the Rams made it back to the Super Bowl. But they fell to the Patriots 13–3. Three years later, the Rams reached the Super Bowl again. This time, they beat the Cincinnati Bengals 23–20. Los Angeles won a thriller on a late touchdown.

PLAYER SPOTLIGHT

KURT WARNER

In the mid-1990s, Kurt Warner was working at a grocery store. He couldn't land a spot on an NFL team. So, he played quarterback in the Arena Football League. Finally, in 1998, the Rams signed him as a backup.

Warner was supposed to be a backup again in 1999. But the team's starting quarterback hurt his knee. Warner took over. And he never looked back. In 1999, he led the NFL with 41 touchdown passes. Warner won the MVP Award that season. He also led the Rams to a Super Bowl win.

KURT WARNER WON HIS SECOND MVP AWARD IN THE 2001 SEASON.

CHAPTER 5

MODERN STARS

Quarterback Kurt Warner led a Rams offense known as the "Greatest Show on Turf." His strong arm helped the Rams set scoring records. Running back Marshall Faulk led the team's ground attack. Faulk wasn't just a great runner. He was also a reliable receiver.

Marshall Faulk (28) topped 1,000 rushing and 1,000 receiving yards in 1999.

Isaac Bruce was the team's best receiver in the late 1990s and early 2000s. Bruce spent 14 years with the Rams. He recorded eight 1,000-yard seasons. Fellow receiver Torry Holt earned seven trips to the Pro Bowl. He topped 1,000 receiving yards eight years in a row.

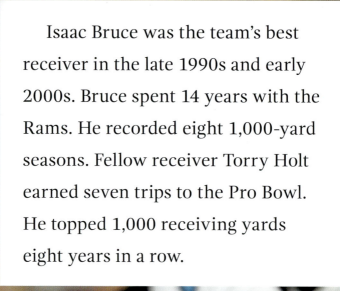

TOUGH TACKLE

The Rams had the first pick in the 1997 draft. They selected offensive tackle Orlando Pace. It turned out to be a great choice. Pace spent 12 seasons with the Rams. He made the Pro Bowl seven years in a row.

Torry Holt led the NFL in receiving yards in 2000 and 2003.

Jalen Ramsey intercepted 10 passes while he played for the Rams.

The Rams drafted defensive tackle Aaron Donald in 2014. He soon became the heart of the team's defense. Cornerback Jalen Ramsey came aboard in 2019. He made the Pro Bowl in each of his four seasons with the Rams. Defensive end Von Miller joined the team in the middle of the 2021 season. Miller had two sacks in the Super Bowl against the Bengals.

In 2021, the Rams traded for quarterback Matthew Stafford. He'd spent 12 years with the Detroit Lions. But he reached new heights in Los Angeles. Wide receiver Cooper Kupp also had a great year in 2021. He led the league in catches. He led in receiving yards and touchdown catches, too.

Cooper Kupp scores the game-winning touchdown in the Super Bowl.

PLAYER SPOTLIGHT

AARON DONALD

The Rams selected Aaron Donald in the first round of the 2014 draft. The defensive tackle quickly became one of the best players in the NFL. In his first season, Donald recorded nine sacks. That helped him win the Defensive Rookie of the Year Award.

Donald played for 10 seasons. He made the Pro Bowl in all 10 of them. He was also named Defensive Player of the Year three times. Donald was at his best when it mattered most. He had two sacks in the Rams' Super Bowl win over Cincinnati.

AARON DONALD RACKED UP 111 SACKS DURING HIS CAREER.

CHAPTER 6

TEAM TRIVIA

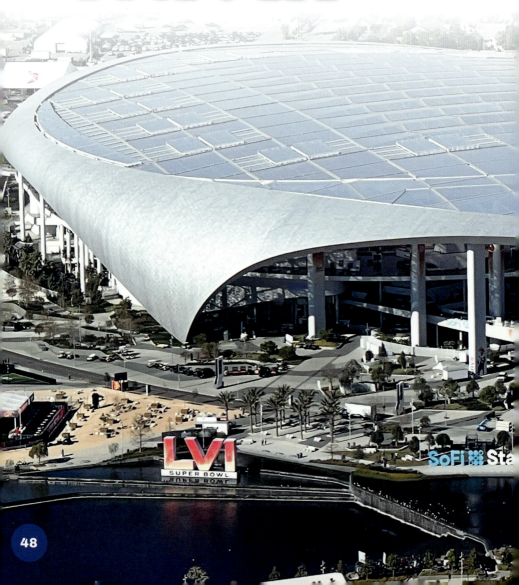

In 2020, a new stadium opened in Los Angeles. Both the Rams and the Los Angeles Chargers began playing there. It wasn't the first time those teams shared a stadium. In 1960, they both played at the Los Angeles Coliseum.

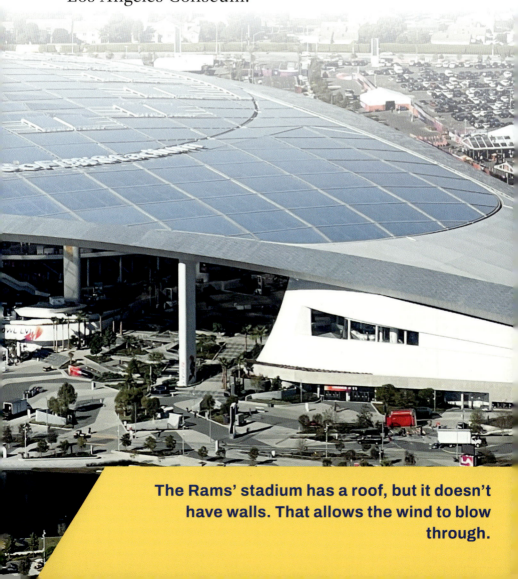

The Rams' stadium has a roof, but it doesn't have walls. That allows the wind to blow through.

From 1934 to 1945, no Black athletes played in the NFL. Team owners wouldn't allow it. The Rams moved to Los Angeles in 1946. The city allowed the Rams to play at the Coliseum. But the city had one demand. The Rams had to allow Black players on the team.

BREAKING BARRIERS

The Rams signed two Black players in 1946. One was running back Kenny Washington. The other was receiver Woody Strode. The two had been teammates in college.

Kenny Washington (13) had the longest run of the 1947 NFL season.

The Rams' helmet design has not changed much since 1948.

Fred Gehrke played running back for the Rams in the late 1940s. He wasn't a big star. However, he helped change the game. Back then, football helmets were plain plastic shells. But Gehrke was an artist. So, he painted the first helmet logo in NFL history. Before long, all Rams players had horns painted on their helmets.

Flipper Anderson (83) led the NFL in yards per catch in 1989 and 1990.

Wide receiver Willie "Flipper" Anderson spent seven years with the Rams. He's best known for a game in 1989. The Rams were facing the New Orleans Saints. Anderson set an NFL record with 336 receiving yards.

NIGHT TRAIN

Dick "Night Train" Lane was one of the greatest defensive backs ever. He joined the Rams in 1952. Lane spent only two seasons with Los Angeles. But he made history. In his rookie season, Lane grabbed 14 interceptions. That set an NFL record.

TEAM RECORDS

All-Time Passing Yards: 23,758
Jim Everett (1986–93)

All-Time Touchdown Passes: 154
Roman Gabriel (1962–72)

All-Time Rushing Yards: 10,138
Steven Jackson (2004–12)

All-Time Receiving Yards: 14,109
Isaac Bruce (1994–2007)

All-Time Interceptions: 46
Eddie Meador (1959–70)

All-Time Sacks: 159.5*
Deacon Jones (1961–71)

All-Time Scoring: 1,223
Jeff Wilkins (1997–2007)

All-Time Coaching Wins: 75
John Robinson (1983–91)

NFL Titles: 2
(1945, 1951)

Super Bowl Titles: 2
(1999, 2021)

Sacks were not an official statistic until 1982. However, researchers have studied old games to determine sacks dating back to 1960.

All statistics are accurate through 2023.

TIMELINE

1936 — The Cleveland Rams play one season in the AFL. They join the NFL the following year.

1945 — The Rams beat Washington to win their first NFL title.

1946 — The Rams move to Los Angeles, California, making it the first West Coast city with a major league sports team.

1951 — In their third straight NFL title game, the Rams finally win, beating the Cleveland Browns.

1973 — The Rams win the first of seven straight division titles.

1979 — In their first Super Bowl appearance, the Rams lose to the Steelers 31–19.

1995 — The Rams move again, this time to St. Louis, Missouri.

1999 — Behind the "Greatest Show on Turf," the Rams win their first Super Bowl by beating the Tennessee Titans.

2016 — The Rams move back to Los Angeles.

2021 — Matthew Stafford hits Cooper Kupp for the game-winning touchdown as the Rams defeat the Cincinnati Bengals in the Super Bowl.

COMPREHENSION QUESTIONS

Write your answers on a separate piece of paper.

1. Write a paragraph that explains the main ideas of Chapter 2.

2. Who do you think was the greatest player in Rams history? Why?

3. Who was quarterback when the Rams won their first Super Bowl?
   - **A.** Norm Van Brocklin
   - **B.** Jim Everett
   - **C.** Kurt Warner

4. How might Rams history be different if Fred Gehrke had not played for the team?
   - **A.** The team would probably have a different helmet design.
   - **B.** The team would probably have more Super Bowl titles.
   - **C.** The team would probably play in a different city.

5. What does **attendance** mean in this book?

   *The stadium could hold more than 100,000 fans. By 1949, the Rams were leading the NFL in **attendance**.*

       A. the number of titles a team wins
       B. the number of fans at a game
       C. the number of teams in a league

6. What does **demand** mean in this book?

   *The city allowed the Rams to play at the Coliseum. But the city had one **demand**. The Rams had to allow Black players on the team.*

       A. a team that moves to a new city
       B. a stadium that holds many fans
       C. a rule that must be followed

Answer key on page 64.

GLOSSARY

arena football
A form of indoor football that takes place on a 50-yard field surrounded by boards.

conference
A group of teams that make up part of a sports league.

division
In the NFL, a group of teams that make up part of a conference.

draft
A system that lets teams select new players coming into the league.

interceptions
Passes that are caught by a defensive player.

league
A group of teams that play one another and compete for a championship.

logo
A team's symbol.

playoffs
A set of games played after the regular season to decide which team is the champion.

rookie
An athlete in his or her first year as a professional player.

sacks
Plays that happen when a defender tackles the quarterback before he can throw the ball.

TO LEARN MORE

BOOKS

Coleman, Ted. *Los Angeles Rams All-Time Greats*. Mendota Heights, MN: Press Box Books, 2022.

Greenberg, Keith Elliot. *Meet Cooper Kupp*. Minneapolis: Lerner Publications, 2023.

Patrick, Lee. *Aaron Donald: Football Star*. Mendota Heights, MN: Focus Readers, 2020.

ONLINE RESOURCES

Visit **www.apexeditions.com** to find links and resources related to this title.

ABOUT THE AUTHOR

Brendan Flynn is a San Francisco resident and an author of numerous children's books. In addition to writing about sports, Flynn also enjoys competing in triathlons, Scrabble tournaments, and chili cook-offs.

INDEX

Anderson, Willie, 55

Bruce, Isaac, 40

Dickerson, Eric, 27
Donald, Aaron, 43, 46

Everett, Jim, 27

Faulk, Marshall, 38
Fears, Tom, 22

Gabriel, Roman, 22
Gehrke, Fred, 53
Grier, Rosey, 24

Hirsch, Elroy, 22
Holt, Torry, 40

Jones, Deacon, 18, 24
Jones, Mike, 31

Kupp, Cooper, 44

Lane, Dick, 55

Lundy, Lamar, 24

Mack, Tom, 27
Miller, Von, 43

Nacua, Puka, 6

Olsen, Merlin, 24

Pace, Orlando, 40

Ramsey, Jalen, 43

Slater, Jackie, 27
Snow, Jack, 22
Stafford, Matthew, 6, 44
Strode, Woody, 50

Van Brocklin, Norm, 20

Warner, Kurt, 36, 38
Washington, Kenny, 50
Waterfield, Bob, 20

Youngblood, Jack, 24

ANSWER KEY:
1. Answers will vary; 2. Answers will vary; 3. C; 4. A; 5. B; 6. C